I0837243

TAM O' SHANTER

A Tale

W.B.

TAM O' SHANTER

A Tale

Robert Burns

Arabi Manor
New Orleans

Printed in the United States and United Kingdom by
Arabi Manor, a Rebel Satori Imprint

"Tam o' Shanter" layout inspired by the E. Arnold of London's 1902 edition.

Extra materials from John Dawson Ross's *All About Tam o' Shanter* publilshed by The Raeburn Book Co. in 1900.

Engravings on pages 16, 29, and 30 produced by I. Price c. 1895; from the Arabi Manor collection.

ISBN: 978-1-60864-191-8

Robert Burns

1759 – 1796

Of Brownyis and of Bogillis full is this Buke.
—Gawin Douglas

TAM O’ SHANTER

HEN CHAPMAN BILLIES LEAVE THE STREET, AND DROUTHY NEIBORS, NEIBORS, MEET; AS MARKET DAYS ARE WEARING LATE, AND FOLK BEGIN TO TAK THE GATE, WHILE WE SIT BOUSING AT THE NAPPY, AN’ GETTING FOU AND UNCO HAPPY, WE THINK NA ON THE LANG SCOTS MILES, THE MOSSES, WATERS, SLAPS AND STILES, THAT LIE BETWEEN US AND OUR HAME, WHERE SITS OUR SULKY, SULLEN DAME, GATHERING HER BROWS LIKE GATHERING STORM, NURSING HER WRATH TO KEEP IT WARM.

THIS truth fand honest Tam o' Shanter,
As he frae Ayr ae night did canter:
(Auld Ayr, wham ne'er a town surpasses,
For honest men and bonie lasses.)

O Tam! had'st thou but been sae wise
As taen thy ain wife Kate's advice!
She tauld thee weel thou was a skellum,
A bletherin, blusterin, drunken blellum;
That frae November till October,
Ae market-day thou was na sober;
That ilka melder wi' the miller,
Thou sat as lang as thou had siller;
That ev'ry naig was ca'd a shoe on,
The smith and thee gat roarin fou on;
That at the Lord's house, ev'n on Sunday,
Thou drank wi' Kirkton Jean till Monday.
She prophesied, that, late or soon,
Thou would be found deep drown'd in Doon;
Ot catch'd wi' warlocks in the mirk,
By Alloway's auld haunted kirk.

AH, gentle dames! it gars me greet,
To think how mony counsels sweet,
How mony lengthen'd sage advices,
The husband frae the wife despises!

BUT to our tale:—Ae market night,
Tam had got planted unco right,
Fast by an ingle, bleezing finely,
Wi' reaming swats that drank divinely;
And at his elbow, Souter Johnie,
His ancient, trusty, drouthy crony:
Tam lo'ed him like a vera brither;
They had been fou for weeks thegither.
The night drave on wi' sangs and clatter;
And ay the ale was growing better:
The landlady and Tam grew gracious
Wi' secret favours, sweet, and precious:
The souter tauld his queerest stories;
The landlord's laugh was ready chorus:
The storm without might rair and rustle,
Tam did na mind the storm a whistle.

CARE, mad to see a man sae happy,
E'en drown'd himsel amang the nappy:
As bees flee hame wi' lades o' treasure,
The minutes wing'd their way wi' pleasure;
Kings may be blest, but Tam was glorious,
O'er a' the ills o' life victorious!

BUT pleasures are like poppies spread,
You seize the flow'r, its bloom is shed;
Or like the snow falls in the river,

A moment white—then melts forever;
Or like the borealis race,
That flit ere you can point their place;
Or like the rainbow's lovely form
Evanishing amid the storm.
Nae man can tether time or tide:
The hour approaches Tam maun ride,—
That hour, o' night's black arch the key-stane
That dreary hour he mounts his beast in;
And sic a night he taks the road in,
As ne'er poor sinner was abroad in.

THE wind blew as 'twad blawn its last;
The rattling show'rs rose on the blast;
The speedy gleams the darkness swallow'd;
Loud, deep, and lang the thunder bellow'd:
That night, a child might understand,
The Deil had business on his hand.

WEEL mounted on his grey mare, Meg,—
A better never lifted leg,—
Tam skelpit on thro' dub and mire,
Despising wind and rain and fire;
Whiles holding fast his guid blue bonnet,
Whiles crooning o'er some auld Scots sonnet,
Whiles glowrin round wi' prudent cares,
Lest bogles catch him unawares.

Kirk-Alloway was drawing nigh,
Whare ghaists and houlets nightly cry.

BY this time he was cross the ford,
Whare in the snaw the chapman smoor'd;
And past the birks and meikle stane,
Whare drucken Charlie brak's neckbane:
And thro' the whins, and by the cairn,
Whare hunters fand the murder'd bairn;
And near the thorn, aboon the well,
Whare Mungo's mither hang'd hersel.
Before him Doon pours all his floods;
The doubling storm roars thro' the woods;
The lightnings flash from pole to pole,
Near and more near the thunders roll;
When, glimmering thro' the groaning trees,
Kirk-Alloway seem'd in a bleeze:
Thro' ilka bore the beams were glancing,
And loud resounded mirth and dancing.

INSPIRING bold John Barleycorn!
What dangers thou can'st make us scorn!
Wi' tippenny we fear nae evil;
Wi' usquebae we'll face the devil!
The swats sae ream'd in Tammie's noddle,
Fair play, he car'd na deils a boddle.
But Maggie stood right sair astonish'd,

Till, by the heel and hand admonish'd,
She ventur'd forward on the light;
And, wow! Tam saw an unco sight!

WARLOCKS and witches in a dance;
Nae cotillion brent-new frae France,
But hornpipes, jigs, strathspeys, and reels
Put life and mettle in their heels.
A winnock bunker in the east,
There sat Auld Nick in shape o' beast:
A towzie tyke, black, grim, and large,
To gie them music was his charge;
He screw'd the pipes and gart them skirl,
Till roof and rafters a' did dirl.—
Coffins stood round like open presses,
That shaw'd the dead in their last dresses;
And by some devilish cantraip sleight
Each in its cauld hand held a light,
By which heroic Tam was able
To note upon the haly table
A murderer's banes in gibbet airns;
Twa span-lang, wee, unchristen'd bairns;
A thief, new-cutted frae the rape—
Wi' his last gasp his gab did gape;
Five tomahawks, wi' blude red-rusted;
Five scimitars, wi' murder crusted;
A garter, which a babe had strangled;

A knife, a father's throat had mangled,
Whom his ain son o' life bereft—
The grey hairs yet stack to the heft;
Wi' mair o' horrible and awfu',
Which ev'n to name wad be unlawfu'.

AS Tammie glowr'd, amaz'd and curious,
The mirth and fun grew fast and furious:
The piper loud and louder blew,
The dancers quick and quicker flew;
They reel'd, they set, they cross'd, they cleekit
Till ilka carlin swat and reekit
And coost her duddies to the wark
And linket at it in her sark!

NOW Tam, O Tam! had thae been queans,
A' plump and strapping in their teens!
Their sarks, instead o' creeshie flannen,
Been snaw-white seventeen hunder linen!—
Thir breeks o' mine, my only pair,
That ance were plush, o' gude blue hair,
I wad hae gien them aff y hurdies,
For ae blink o' the bonie burdies!

BUT wither'd beldams, auld and droll,
Rigwoodie hags wad spean a foal,
Lowping and flinging on a crummock.

I wonder didna turn thy stomach.

BUT Tam ken'd what was what fu' brawlie;
There was ae winsom wench and walie,
That night enlisted in the core
(Lang after ken'd on Carrick shore.
For mony a beast to dead she shot,
And perish'd mony a bonie boat,
And shook baith meikle corn and bear,
And kept the country-side in fear);
Her cutty sark o' Paisley harn,
That while a lassie she had worn,
In longitude tho' sorely scanty,
It was her best, and she was vauntie.
Ah! little ken'd thy reverend grannie,
That sark she coft for her wee Nannie,
Wi' twa pund Scots ('twas a' her riches),
Wad ever grac'd a dance of witches!

BUT here my Muse her wing maun cow'r,
Sic flights are far beyond her pow'r;
To sing how Nannie lap and flang,
(A souple jad she was and strang),
And how Tam stood like ane bewitch'd,
And thought his very een enrich'd;
Even Satan glowr'd and fidg'd fu' fain,
And hotch'd and blew wi' might and main:

Till first ae caper, syne anither,
Tam tint his reason a' thegither,
And roars out, "Weel done, Cutty-sark!"
And in an instant all was dark:
And scarcely had he Maggie rallied,
When out the hellish legion sallied.

AS bees bizz out wi' angry fyke,
When plundering herds assail their byke;
As open pussie's mortal foes,
When, pop! she starts before their nose;
As eager runs the market-crowd,
When "Catch the thief!" resounds aloud;
So Maggie runs, the witches follow,
Wi' mony an eldritch skriech and hollo.

AH, Tam! ah, Tam! thou'll get thy fairin!
In hell they'll roast thee like a herrin!
In vain thy Kate awaits thy comin!
Kate soon will be a woefu' woman!
Now, do thy speedy utmost, Meg,
And win the key-stane of the brig:
There at them thou thy tail may toss,
A running stream they dare na cross.
But ere the key-stane she could make,
The fient a tail she had to shake!
For Nannie far before the rest,

Hard upon noble Maggie prest,
And flew at Tam wi' furious ettle;
But little wist she Maggie's mettle—
Ae spring brought aff her master hale
But left behind her ain grey tail:
The carlin claught her by the rump,
And left poor Maggie scarce a stump.

NOW, wha this tale o' truth shall read,
Ilk man and mother's son, take heed,
Whene'er to drink you are inclin'd,
Or cutty-sarks run in your mind,
Think, ye may buy the joys o'er dear,
Remember Tam o' Shanter's mear.

CONTENTS

WHEN CHAPMAN BILLIES LEAVE THE STREET, AND DROUTHY NEIBORS, NEIBORS, MEET; AS MARKET DAYS ARE WEARING LATE, AND FOLK BEGIN TO TAK THE GATE, WHILE WE SIT BOUSING AT THE NAPPY, AN' GETTING FOU AND UNCO HAPPY, WE THINK NA ON THE LANG SCOTS MILES, THE MOSSES, WATERS, SLAPS AND STILES, THAT LIE BETWEEN US AND OUR HAME, WHERE SITS OUR SULKY, SULLEN DAME, GATHERING HER BROWS LIKE GATHERING STORM, NURSING HER WRATH TO KEEP IT WARM.

of that choice spirit, Souter Johnny—Shoemaker Johnny—his companion in many a long carouse. So the souter was beguiled from his last, and the congenial pair straight-way betook themselves to their favorite inn, where a warm welcome and the best of "yill" awaited them. When the evening closed in Tam found himself snugly seated at a fireside far more dear to him than his own and almost as familiar—the souter at his elbow, convulsing him with the queerest stories ; a jolly boniface supplying him with foaming draughts of powerful Scotch ale ; and a buxom landlady beaming upon him through fragrant tobacco-mists. Never was the souter more deliciously droll never did ale taste better ; never was the landlord's laugh more unctuous or the landlady's smile more gracious—she was a much more agreeable woman, Tam could not help thinking, than Mrs. Graham. And Tam made the most of the occasion. Like the truant boy at the circus, he took no thought of the reckoning to come. Sufficient for the hour was the enjoyment thereof. His zest was as great as though the revelry were taking place under his own roof-tree, with the sanction of a compliant wife. Nay, it was greater, for is it not the fruit which is forbidden that most delights the human palate ? In his boisterous gayety Tarn heeded not the specter which obtruded upon the feast. But we may be sure that the specter became more menacing as the evening advanced ; that she took on the form and manner of his objurgatory spouse ; that she dropped her poison, in increasing doses, into every cup ; that she jealously interrupted his delightful tête-à-tête with his comely hostess ; that she whispered in his ear of the long and dismal ride to come, with a curtain-lecture of more than or- dinary length and bitterness at the end ; and that at last, when the dreaded hour of midnight arrived, she pointed imperiously to the door and bade him begone! We may easily fancy the drunk but docile farmer as he "stachered out" in obedience to the mandate and floundered into the saddle, his jovial host standing ready with a stirrup-cup (supplementary to the *doch an doris*) ; the repeated admonitions screamed from the doorway by the anxious hostess ; the concerted farewell ; and the parting joke flung after him by the inexhaustible souter, as Meg started on her record-breaking run.

When Tam cleared the friendly shelter of the town and reached the open country, he found himself at the mercy of the wildest storm that ever blew in Scotland—at least in his generation.

The Banks of the Doon

The lightning flared, the thunder crashed, the rain rattled, and the wind howled. The farmer's homeward course lay past the scene of many a dreadful story, told late at night by smouldering peat fires to shuddering listeners. Here an unfortunate pedler had perished miserably in the snow ; a little farther on, where a huge rock stood near a clump of birch trees, a drunk- en "ne'er-do-weel" had broken his useless neck ; some distance farther on a party of hunters had one day found a murdered babe ; on yet farther was an abandoned well, guarded by an aged hawthorn tree, where a wretched old crone had hanged herself. But the most fearsome landmark of all was Kirk Alloway ; a little, old, ruined church near a bridge, spanning the river Doon, over which Tam had to cross. Any old wife could tell you that this was the worst haunted place in all Scotland. It is probable that as Tam charged headlong through the inferno of warring elements, his confused wits busy with excuses to be offered to the frowning Kate, he wished himself well past this dreaded spot. Emerging at length from an adjacent wood into full view of the once-sacred edifice, he looked anxiously toward it and beheld a spectacle that might well have frozen the blood of any man whose veins were not superheated by "guid Scotch drink." The old church was ablaze with a weird light, streaming from candles held in the rigid hands of dead men, who stood in open coffins ranged against the walls ; and through the doorless doorway and the windowless casements he beheld a concourse of warlocks and witches dancing like mad about a long table, on which was displayed an assortment of corpses and other cheerful objects. The music proceeded from a huge black animal, the shape of a dog and the size of a bear, ensconced in a windowseat at the eastern extremity of the kirk ; which Tam knew instinctively to be the great enemy of mankind himself—for surely no one else could have played the bagpipes with such unearthly skill. Drink had made Tam insensible to fear. Instead of fleeing as a sober man would have done, he rode boldly forward. The facetiously inclined may see in this another point of similarity between the heroes of Burns and Irving, and declare that Tam here showed the same quality that distinguished the imperturbable Rip Van Winkle in his colloquy with the ghostly pirates, namely, Dutch courage. The hard ride and the startling character of his adventure had partially cleared his brain, but the scene before him affected his senses with a new madness.

It is related of the poet Longfellow that when he returned to America in the early forties, "he found the world drunken with the grace of Fanny Elssler." It was this species of intoxication which now seized upon Tam. For prominent in the dance—her beauty and shapeliness accentuated by her gruesome surroundings—was a young and graceful witch possessed of extraordinary strength and agility. Her attire was of the scantiest, and in her wild abandon she executed such astounding leaps, bounds, and pirouettes as would have made any opera premiere, or even the adored Elssler herself, turn green with envy. Tam became so enthusiastic at her performance that he involuntarily applauded—and betrayed his presence. Instantly the lights were extinguished, and forth upon the midnight air, their phosphorescent forms gleaming through the darkness, came the whole infernal host, all eager to fasten their clutches on the unhappy mortal who had dared to disturb their orgies. Tam wheeled his horse and made for the bridge. Any one versed in the folk-lore of Scotland will tell you that if you are pursued under like circumstances and you can manage to reach the middle of a running stream, you are safe—the arch-fiend himself is powerless against you. The keystone of the bridge became, therefore, Tam's objective point ; and to it he urged his sturdy mare with voice, whip, and spur.

Under the influence of terror Meg developed a speed that might easily have won her the Derby. But the poor beast was not striving against earthly competitors. Nannie, the athletic witch, showed herself as superior in the chase as in the dance, and gained most appallingly on poor Tam. Horse, rider, and witch reached the bridge at almost the same instant ; and just as Meg was in the act of clearing the keystone the witch caught her by the tail, which instantly came off in the infernal grasp as though blasted by a lightning stroke. But the mischief ended here. The river Doon now lay between the baffled demons and their intended victim. The tailless Maggie and her now thoroughly sobered master finished their homeward journey in safety ; and it is to be hoped that, as water had proved to be Tam's salvation on this occasion, he was partial to it ever afterward.

WITCH STORIES

RELATING TO ALLOWAY KIRK.

BY ROBERT BURNS.

"AMONG the witch stories which I have heard relating to Alloway Kirk," said the poet in a letter to Captain Grose, "I distinctly remember only two or three. Upon a stormy night, amid whistling squalls of wind and bitter blasts of hail—in short, on such a night as the devil would choose to take the air in—a farmer or a farmer's servant was plodding and plashing homeward with the plough-irons on his shoulder, having been getting some repairs on them at a neighbouring smithy. His way lay by the Kirk of Alloway, and being rather on the anxious look-out in approaching the place, so well known to be a favorite haunt of the devil, and the devil's friends and emissaries, he was struck aghast by discovering, through the horrors of the stormy night, a light which on his nearer approach plainly showed itself to proceed from the haunted edifice. Whether he had been fortified from above on his devout supplication, as is customary with people when they suspect the immediate presence of Satan, or whether according to another custom, he had got courageously drunk at the smithy, I will not pretend to determine ; but so it was that he ventured to go up to—nay, into the very kirk. As luck would have it his temerity came off unpunished. The members of the infernal junto were all out on some midnight business or other, and he saw nothing but a kind of kettle or caldron depending from the roof over the fire, simmering some heads of unchristened children, limbs of malefactors, etc., for the business of the night. It was in for a penny in a pound with the honest ploughman, so without ceremony he unhooked the caldron from off the fire and pouring out its damnable ingredients, inverted it on his head and carried it fairly home, where it remained long in the family a living evidence of the truth of the story.

"Another story which I can prove to be equally authentic was as follows:

"On a market day in the town of Ayr, a farmer from Carrick, and consequently whose way lay by the very gate of Alloway kirkyard, in order to cross the river Doon at the old bridge, which is about two or three hundred yards farther on than the said gate, had been detained by his business, till by the time he reached Alloway it was the wizard hour, between night and morning.

"Though he was terrified with a blaze streaming from the kirk, yet as it is a well-known fact that to turn back on these occasions is running by far the greatest risk of mischief, he prudently advanced on his road. When he had reached the gate of the kirkyard, he was surprised and entertained through the ribs and arches of an old Gothic window, which still faces the highway, to see a dance of witches merrily footing it round their old sooty blackguard master, who was keeping them all alive with the power of his bagpipe. The farmer stopping his horse to observe them a little, could plainly descry the faces of many old women of his acquaintance and neighborhood. How the gentleman was dressed tradition does not say, but the ladies were all in their smocks ; and one of them happening unluckily to have a smock which was considerably too short to answer all the purposes of that piece of dress, our farmer was so tickled that he involuntarily burst out with a loud laugh: "Weel luppen, Maggie wi' the short sark!" and recollecting himself, instantly spurred his horse to the top of his speed. I need not mention the universally known fact that no diabolical power can pursue you beyond the middle of a running stream. Luckily it was for the poor farmer that the river Doon was so near, for notwithstanding the speed of his horse which was a good one, against he reached the middle of the arch of the bridge, and consequently the middle of the stream the pursuing vengeful hags were so close at his heels, that one of them actually sprang to seize him, but it was too late, nothing was on her side of the stream but the horse's tail, which immediately gave way at her infernal grip, as if blasted by a stroke of lightning, but the farmer was beyond her reach. However the unsightly tailless condition of the vigorous steed was to the last hour of the noble creature's life, an awful warning to the Carrick farmers not to stay too late in Ayr markets.

"The last relation I shall give, though equally true, is not so well identified as the two former with regard to the scene, but as the best authorities give it for Alloway, I shall relate it.

"On a summer's evening about the time nature has put on her sables to mourn the expiry of the cheerful day, a shepherd-boy belonging to a farm in the immediate neighborhood of Alloway Kirk, had just folded his charge and was returning home. As he passed the kirk, in the adjoining field, he fell in with a crowd of men and women who were busy pulling stems of the plant ragwort. He observed that as each person pulled a ragwort, she or he got astride of it and called out, ' up horsie!' on which the ragwort flew off, like Pegasus through the air with its rider. The foolish boy likewise pulled his ragwort, and cried with the rest, 'up horsie!' and strange to tell, away he flew with the company. The first stage at which the cavalcade stopt was a merchant's wine cellar in Bordeaux, where without saying by your leave, they quaffed away at the best the cellar could afford until the morning, foe to the imps and works of darkness, threatened to throw light on the matter, and frightened them away from their carousals.

"The poor shepherd lad being equally a stranger to the scene and liquor, heedlessly got himself drunk, and when the rest took horse, he fell asleep, and was found so next day by some of the people belonging to the merchant. Somebody that understood Scotch asking him what he was, he said, such a one's herd in Alloway, and by some means or other getting home again, he lived to tell the world the wondrous tale.

“This letter is interesting,” says Alexander Smith, as showing the actual body of tradition on which Burns had to work—the soil out of which the consummate poem grew like a flower. And it is worthy of notice also how out of the letter, some of the best things in the poem have come ; ‘such a night as the devil would choose to take the air in’, being for instance, the suggestion of the couplet,

That night a child might understand,
The Deil had business on his hand.

It is pleasant to know that Burns thought well of ‘Tam o’ Shanter’.”

HOW TAM O' SHANTER CAME TO BE WRITTEN.

BY GILBERT BURNS.

WHEN my father fe*u*eed his little property near Alloway Kirk, the wall of the churchyard had gone to ruin, and cattle had free liberty of pasture in it. My father with two or three neighbors joined in an application to the Town Council of Ayr, who were superiors of the adjoining land, for liberty to rebuild it, and raised by subscription a sum for enclosing this ancient cemetery with a wall ; hence he came to consider it as his burial place, and we learned that reverence for it that people generally have for the burial place of their ancestors. My brother was living at Ellisland when Captain Grose, on his peregrinations through Scotland, stayed some time at Carse House, in the neighborhood, with Captain Robert Biddell of Glenriddle, a particular friend of my brother's. The antiquarian and the poet were 'unco pack and thick thegither'. Robert requested of Captain Grose, when he should come to Ayrshire, that he would make a drawing of Alloway Kirk, as it was the burial place of his father, and where he himself had a sort of claim to lay down his bones when they should be no longer serviceable to him, and added by way of encouragement, that it was the scene of many a good story of witches and apparitions—of which he knew the Captain was very fond. The Captain agreed to the request, provided the poet would furnish a witch story to be printed along with it. '"Tam o' Shanter" was produced on this occasion and was first published in *Grose's Antiquities of Scotland.*

Robert Burns Birthplace

Alloway Kirk

AT ALLOWAY'S HAUNTED KIRK.

BY the roadside at the foot of the narrow steps which ascend to Alloway's ancient kirk-yard, two people, who may be called the Ramblers, stumbled upon a blind beggar and a wide-awake dog. It was a dog remarkable in many ways ; it was white on a muddy day, sleek and well-nourished, intelligent and altogether unlike the cowed animal tethered to the blind by a leading string. The Ramblers having bestowed a "collection" and received thanks glibly wagged off tongue and tail, mounted the steep steps to explore. They saw right in front of them a picturesque figure meditating among the tombs. Simultaneously a whispered desire to sketch the old man passed between the misguided visitors, when the intended subject of pen-and-pencil attentions slowly raised his voice and his long forefinger. We stood beside the grave of the poet's relatives—a swift look at the tombstone had already intimated as much to the Ramblers, but they murmured thanks for the information. After a minute or so Tam o' Shanter stalked on to an ancient, dilapidated stone and again lifted his voice in monotone ; the coarse Tarn o' Shanter bonnet was drawn well down over one side of his wrinkled brow, his gray-blue eye proclaimed the true Scot ; the increasing flow of carefully chosen descriptive language gradually enlightened the Ramblers who had innocently believed his appearance to be accidental ; it dawned on them that they were in the hands of a guide, and a character. On he stalked through the slippery places ; he was in his element, his tongue rolled but with precision the histories of the grass-grown graves with only a rude device partly visible as the key to his harangue. Here was the burial-place of this and that noble family ; one dead and gone dame's fate elicited an emphatic opinion from him. "It wis a great peety, she wis a fine leddy. Te noo staun foment the grave o' Souter Johnny, deed div ye," said the old man, "an' noo tak' a look ahint ye at the kirk." The Ramblers did so ; they saw a great tree at the side of the ruined kirk wall, and, half in and half out of the church a stone baptismal font which had received its water from a little stream outside. "Rabbie Burns wis bapteezed oot o' it, an' jist anither bairn efter him, deed wis he, " quoth the latter-day Tam o' Shanter. The Ramblers gazed curiously in at what had once been Alloway Kirk, and heard as in a dream who had last 'ineenistered' therein ; but all of a sudden a change was observed to come over the guide, he drew himself up to the limit of his inches, swung his long arms to and fro pendlumwise and began to recite "Tam o' Shanter" in the drollest way imaginable. One Rambler's mind was debating on what the consequences of stopping the swinging arms would be ; the other was thinking how strange it was for this old character, in whom mischief -loving Rabbie Burns would have gloried, to be repeating the imaginative lines of Scotland's dearest poet within a stone's cast of where the genius was received into the visible church by the sprinkling of water. In the midst of these natural thoughts the voice ceased with a snap, and the arms stopped with a jerk, and the eye, the eye under the Tam o' Shanter's droop, took an expression which meant toll or—a bit of Tam's mind. An irresistible desire to laugh outright at this jump from the poetry to the prose of life seized the Ramblers, but was sternly repressed. Tam's horny hand was crossed with silver and he took up his meditative position once more among the tombs. Farther down the road a little time was spent in the whitewashed kitchen where the Ploughman-Poet was born. The table was richly carved—with initials ; the window ledge—such a tiny window—was spluttered with ink from visitor's pens ; the chairs, at least one of them, had cord tied so that it might not he sat upon. Verily a simple, but hallowed place! Driving towards Ayr, a little later, the eyes of the Ramblers fell on a small but interesting procession hobbling and chuckling homeward. It consisted of a blind beggar, a frisky-dog, and Tam o' Shanter. The three were in solemn league and covenant!

TAM O' SHANTER.

FROM "BURNS AND THE KIRK"

BY ALEXANDER WEBSTBR.

TAM o' Shanter" may be regarded as the sequel to "The Holy Fair." The purpose of the latter is the exposure of the gross desecration recurrent in the precincts of the house of God, and of the profanation of the Sacrament by sensuality, hypocrisy, and revelry ; the inner intention of the former being an exposure of the baleful superstition regarding supernatural evil beings, fostered by the Church in the name of religion. "Tam o' Shanter" shows a desecration of the kirk itself by the midnight dance therein of "warlocks and witches" to the music of the devil. In "The Holy Fair" we are not taken into the Kirk, nor does the devil appear on the scene, though "Black Russell" speaks loudly of the "vast, unbottomed, boundless pit, filled fou o' lowan brumstane. " The carnival goes on outside the kirk, though within touch of it. But in "Tam o' Shanter" we are shown the interior of the kirk, with "Auld Nick" piping in the "winnock-bunker in the east," president of the witches' orgie. One may easily imagine the orgie taking place in the Kirk of Mauchline, on the night of the Holy Fair. To have placed it there would only have been to extend the Fair, and have it taken up, as the night wore on and the day revelers had gone, inside the kirk, by creatures from the "boundless pit." The revel, so placed, would have been a fitting sequel to the profanity of the Fair, and some of "the godly," searching for another "jar," might have been represented as seeing it. But the scene was not so planned by Burns ; and we take it as we find it, and see in it a parable of superstition of the most instructive kind.

The poem originated in a friendly bargain of the author with Captain Grose, the antiquary ; Burns undertaking to supply a witch or ghost story relating to Kirk Alloway if the Captain would include the kirk in his work on Scottish Antiquities. Burns set to work to fulfil his part of the compact on a bright autumn day in 1790. He was then at Ellisland, and went out with writing materials to "a broomy ridge by the river side" which was "a much-frequented haunt" of his, and wrote the poem in "one continuous fit of inspiration." It was a wondrous day's work! It is told as "an ascertained fact" that his wife (anxious, no doubt, to know what engrossing theme detained him so long) discovered him in "an agony of laughter, reciting aloud certain lines of the poem which he had just conceived, the tears in the mean-time rolling down his cheeks ; and that she withdrew from the neighhorhood for a moment, along with her children, that they might not interrupt his ecstasy."

Whatever rank we may give this poem relatively to the other poems of Burns, it must ever appear to us as a marvelous production ; and whether we enter into the spirit of its humor, or hush our mirth at the thrilling touch of its passages of sublime pathos, we feel recreated and instructed on reading or listening to the reading of the poem.

The tale, as is well known, turns upon the tarrying of its hero by the change-house "ingle bleezing finely," enjoying "the reaming swats, that drank divinely." The "unco sight" of "warlocks and witches in a dance," the catastrophe to his mare, the narrow escape of Shanter himself from the witchly clutch—all arise out of the too-freely-quaffed "nappy," and the moral is obvious. But it has been charged against Burns that his poems and songs encourage drinking ; and that even where, as in this poem, he makes plain the dangers of drink, he throws such a glamor over the act of getting fou that it is attractive. It may be said here, in passing, that in such poems as "Scotch Drink," "The Earnest Cry," etc., Burns only drew drinking pictures true to life in his day, and sang the common feeling with regard to drink. And when he becomes the advocate of drink it is of the social glass, with which there is flow of sympathy, and not of sensuous solitary drinking for the love of drink. And in his songs of drink it is the same, the drinking is permeated with good fellowship. In fact, it is the fellowship and not the drinking that he glorifies.

In "Tam o' Shanter" he paints the drinking-scene graphically. There is a coziness and cantinessand jollity about it which is catching; but the feeling is plainly delusive. Tam "was glorious, o^er a' the ills o' life victorious;" but it was in sensuous stupidity. The souter's "queerest stories," the landlady's "favors," "the landlord's laugh," were but "phantasmagoria and many-colored spectra" that deluded as they delighted. With all their jollity, Tam and "his ancient, trusty, drouthy crony" are fools, and that is made evident enough. They sit between landlord and landlady as in a snare, and the wiles of the "nappy" are plied 'round about them till sense and cash are gone. Happy as they are, we are made to feel that they are so at the expense of everything truly manly ; that the brain of the drinker is debased while it is dazzled. Though there is a true touch of humanity in their comradeship, their indulgence of sensuous appetite dehumanizes ; and we see that if they meet as men they part as sots. There is not a single word or suggestion in the poem that is drink-enticing. Even the invocation of "John Barleycorn" tells against his power. The scorn of dangers which he inspires is an illusion. To say nothing of the wife left in the neglect which begets wrath, or of the unco sight in the bleezing kirk, or even the moral at the end of the poem, all of which tell against drinking—that piece of natural and exquisite pathos introduced as anti-climax to Tam's gloriousness is enough to show the folly of such glory :

"But pleasures are like poppies spread," etc.

In "Tam o' Shanter" (whatever may be the case in other pieces) the moral drift is reformatory. The poet honestly describes the drinking custom, credits it with all the sensuous enjoyment belonging to it ; but confronts it with higher things, reveals its subterranean connections, and passes a judgment against it which is impressed with divine sanction.

But all the other scenes in the drama only lead up to the great scene in "Alloway's auld haunted kirk." It was the kirk which the poet had in his mind's eye all the while, according to the bargain with Captain Grose. Most cunningly and profoundly is the scene laid therein, and with a deep religious purpose. The auld haunted kirk furnished him with a habitation wherein to place on view the objects which superstition, supported by religious authority, set up before the imagination. He knew well how orthodoxy made an ally of the devil and his imps, and held the people in terror through them. He was aware of the way in which the underworld had been peopled with all manner of evil spirits, and how even the air of common life had been filled with bodiless creatures of malignant influence. He knew how terrified most people were in the darkness, how they trembled at any strange sound, how completely they were the victims of their own ignorant fears. And he realized how much the Church was to blame for this, how it had prevented the investigation of natural phenomena, hindered the exercise of reason, and rooted its authority in superstition. He perceived how "preachers of the Gospel" had used the fear of the devil as a strong inducement to the outward observances of religion and how they had enhanced their authority by "their supposed ability to counteract this fearful adversary" And so he felt that something effective needed to be done, to deliver men from these superstitions.

In his "Address to the Deil" he plainly spoke a liberating word, and delivered the soul from ^'the hangman's whip." In "Tam o' Shanter" he pursues the same purpose, and boldly seats the devil in the kirk, with all his hellish brood around him, to show religion the objects of its superstition.

The placing of the "towzie tyke" in the winnock-bunker in the east of the Auld Kirk to superintend the dance of "warlocks and witches" was no mere fiction imagined to scare one in whose "noddle" the "swats reamed," but was a matter-of-fact gathering 'round the pulpit of the hellish beings of fearsome creation. There was no more fitting place for the humorous exposure of the progeny of superstition than the kirk itself. The evil brood were born and bred under Church influence, and the parentage had to be brought home to it, so that it might put them to dissolution. With the very sublimity of Burns gathered "the devil and bis angels" in the kirk, and with them all the terrors of death, and then bade men look in to see the sight. As if emerging from its own floor or oozing out of its own atmosphere, there appeared in the "haunted kirk," at the call of the wizard-poet, the ugsome creatures of darkness, the hideous things of the grave, the denizens of hell, the seething spawn of superstition. The kirk becomes Tophet, Hades, Gehenna, hell. Many a time had the walls echoed with talk of such things, often had the preacher pictured such beings to terrified hearers, frequently had "the ill place" been opened in imagination to clinch "the offer of salvation ;" but in the poem, as if the very walls had given back the words, and they had become flesh, the hellish beings themselves come into life in the kirk, and hold their unholy revel on the sacred floor! The Church could hardly have been prepared for such an invasion ; but it was the just reaction of religious superstition, and it could not consistently refuse to look at the ugsome creatures with whom it had made its members familiar. And to look at them in the light of common sense was to be convicted of superstition. In that light they were seen to be creatures of fancy, begotten of ignorance and terror ; and which had no existence in fact whatever. To disabuse the mind of the mischievous fancy was, no doubt, one of the objects that Burns had in writing this poem. He knew well that religion was corrupted by it ; that the darkness, which was God's as well as the light, was made terrible to men through it ; that knowledge of the causes of strange phenomena was hindered by it ; and that the enslaving power of the clergy was maintained by it. And so he set his humor to work, and made men able to laugh at the gross images of their own creation.

To help us to understand the work that he had to do in dissolving the fancy of witchcraft and the general superstition existent regarding unknown forces in action around men, we must know something of the ideas then current concerning "warlocks and witches." Looking back from the earliest case of real importance in the prosecution of witches, Walter Scott says : "For many years the Scottish nation had been remarkable for a credulous belief in witchcraft." The idea underlying the belief was the existence of the devil. He, it was thought, purchased the services of persons whose bodies and souls he bought for some payment or other. These were, at his command and by his power, the instruments of all mischief and everything termed evil.

Everything mysterious of a baleful kind was regarded as witchery. When anything inexplicable happened to man or beast it was a witch who did it. If a field were blighted or weeds come up in the crop, it was some spiteful warlock's doing. If a child fell sick or a woman miscarried it was the effect of some "evil eye." Whatever occurred by accident or misfortune was attributed to witchcraft. Witches could, by Satanic skill, take the shape of frogs, cats, hares, crows, spectres of all kinds. They had, it was supposed, power over all the elements: they could ride on the winds, travel in the air, or run underground. And everything was at their mercy—crops, property, and life itself. By means of them the devil was able to be omnipresent, and to carry out his perpetual malignity against the Infinite Goodness.

The first case of witchcraft in Scotland, of which an account is preserved, is that of the case of the "Earl of Max, brother of James III. of Scotland, who fell under the King's suspicion for consulting with witches and sorcerers how to shorten the King's days. On such a charge, very inexplicably stated, the unhappy Mar was bled to death in his own lodgings without either trial or conviction ; immediately after which catastrophe twelve women of obscure rank, and three or four wizards, or warlocks, as they were termed, were burnt at Edinburgh to give a color to the Earl's guilt." After that, cases of witches prosecuted to death are recorded in great numbers. These, as Scott declares, present a "certain monotony." A curious case, typical of others, occurred in Dumfriesshire half-a-century or so before the birth of Burns. One Bessie Kennedy was tried by the Kirk-Session of Tinwald on a charge of having cursed the horse of one John Carruthers on a certain Sabbath, and wished that it might shoot to dead ; and, further, with having, when the said John told her that his horse had fallen sick through her malignity, "wished that the shoot of dead might light on him and it both" (that is, that he and it might perish by some fatal internal lapse, or "schute," of the system.) The charge was not proved, and Bessie was dismissed ; being warned, however, to exercise "greater watchfulness for the future." It was cases of that kind that suggested to Burns the line in "Tam o' Shanter"— "For mony a beast to dead she shot." Kate Steen or Stephen, who, it is thought, is the person represented under the character of "Cutty Sark," was "an inoffensive but peculiar woman ; of diminutive stature and sometimes of strange attire ; of vagrant but industrious habits ; who carried her 'rock and spindle' with her from house to house to spin ; and was kindly, or at least civilly, received everywhere, from fear, perhaps, of her reputed supernatural gifts as much as from affection."

Now, in the fact of Elatie's "peculiarity" we come upon the secret of the fancy of witchcraft. If a woman happened to be in any way "peculiar" in feature, dress, or habit she was thought to be a witch. And the curious thing is that, when the peculiarity consisted of an unusual heightening of some feature or faculty ; such as unusually large and bright eyes, extraordinary fluency of speech, unusual skill of hand, or uncommon knowledge of any kind, it was set down to witchcraft.

Those who were regarded as witches mostly belonged to the lower classes ; and, when we remember that it was in feudal times that the prosecution of witches was most prevalent in this country, we may conclude that those charged with witchcraft were generally independent, far-seeing, courageous women who took the liberty to reprove the evil doings of those above them. They were the social protestants and insurgents of their day, impelled to speak and act against the powers that kept the people down. By analyzing the reports of the trials of witches in Scotland, we find that either some of the gentry, some laird or lady, or some officious magnate of the law in the interest of the aristocracy was the complainant ; and the charge was generally that of shooting at a laird, or having bewitched the laird's affections, or of meddling in some way with the property of the well-to-do. Walter Scott says—"The gentry hated witches, because the diseases and death of their relations and children were often imputed to them." We may infer, therefore, that those supposed to be witches were women of uncommon appearance and power, more talented than was usual with women of their station ; women of extraordinary energy and insight, who, with startling boldness or with careful but ominous speech, spoke against the wrongs they saw and felt.

The same thing applies to wizards, or warlocks. It appears that they were not so numerous as witches, but they were generally men who had an extraordinary insight into nature—men of humble rank endowed with an extra amount of common sense, curiosity, and intelligence ; who delighted in the investigation of natural things. They were, in fact the scientists of their time. But they were dreaded. They were seen to take to do with stones, plants, and animals in a way that was not canny ; to explore the rocks, the woods, and the pools, and to have their houses full of strange things. And they were not only social protestants but theological protestants : heretic, infidels, men who went not to church, nor held the common religious ideas. Quite a large number of charges against warlocks consist of such things as these—"Circulating pretended prophecies to the unsettlement of the State, and the endangering of the King's title ;" enquiring into the date of the King's birth, anticipating his death, etc. We may judge by that that the warlocks were simply the radicals of their time ; men who, when 'twas treason to think and speak freely, had dared to go beyond political and social orthodoxy. We find among other charges the charge of "breaking and destroying crosses" brought against warlocks, and that shows us that the warlocks were religious reformers. There can be no doubt that the enmity shown by the ecclesiastical powers against "warlocks and witches" is to be accounted for by the fact that the persons supposed to be in league with Satan were heterodox in thought and conduct. In these days ecclesiastical authority was very strict. It was ordained then by "the civil magistrate " (in

Aberdeen at least) "That nae man sail keep from observin and keein the sermonis and prechingis on the ouik days : to set Tuesday and Thursday for hearing of the Word of God, and Christian evangell treulie prechit. Maisters of households, their wyfte, bairns, and servants and other inhabitants, cum to discretion of years, should be catechised every Thursday." If a man had some doubt about the "treulie prechingis," or expressed some skeptical opinion regarding "the Word of God," he was liable to be regarded as a warlock ; and if a woman stayed at home to nurse a sick child or to perform some needful domestic duty in- stead of going to the "prechingis," she was likely to be looked upon as a witch.

In fact, all who in any way spoke against or disobeyed the ecclesiastical ordinance were liable to be dragged to the stake. These ordinances were, therefore, felt to be very oppressive, and there was much insubordination in connection with them. This was the case especially with regard to the Sabbath, which was strictly kept. The revolt against it led to the idea of the "witches' Sabbath." It was thought that those who were regarded as witches, not being at church, were away having a meeting by themselves ; and there is a curious confession of a woman to the effect that the witches when they met were so numerous that "they were told off into squads, or covines, as they were termed, to each of which were appointed two officers. One of them was called the maiden of the covine, and was usually, like Tam o' Shanter's Nannie, a girl of personal attractions, whom Satan placed beside himself, and treated with particular attention. . . . The ceremonial of the Sabbath meetings was very strict. The Foul Fiend was very rigid in exacting the most ceremonious attention from his votaries, and the title of Lord when addressed by them."

The ideas originated in connection with Sabbath superstition, and the Church took care to show by means of them that the devil's Sabbath was as severe as that of the Church. And it also prejudiced the people in favor of its own practices by fostering the fancy that the witches at their Sabbath meeting dug up the bodies of unchristened infants in order to use the materials of them for their sorceries. The moral was plain—have your children christened and then the witches will not get them. It is likely that the idea of the witches' Sabbath rose up out of the condemned practice of walking on the Sabbath—a practice which sensible and courageous people kept up in spite of the censure of the Church.

It is the shame of Calvinism in this country that it was the cause of the humming of thousands of innocent and highly virtuous persons as witches. Under its favor witch-hunting became a trade, and we read of one Hopkins, who, along with a male and female assistant, went up and down the country discovering witches. His usual price was "twenty shillings a town," and for that sum he and his assistants undertook to hunt down all the witches in it. "His principal mode of discovery was to strip the accused persons naked, and thrust pins into various parts of their body, to discover the witch's mark." If this failed, he tied the great toes and thumbs of his victim together, wrapped her in a sheet, and dragged her through a pond or river. If she floated she was a witch, and was put to death. He also kept the persons put into his power waking till they were made mad, or he dragged them about till, by extreme weariness, and the pain of blistered feet, they were glad to confess having the power of witchery. We need not wonder that poor, infirm, sensitive women, stripped naked and tortured, declared that they were actually in league with Satan. Nor is it to be wondered at that others who had gifts for which they could not account admitted the possibility of their being inspired by the devil. Admissions of the kind were extorted over and over again from the hapless creatures who fell under the persecution of the Church.

But in order fully to comprehend what there is in the "warlocks and witches" as they are shown to us by Burns, dancing in "Alloway's auld haunted kirk," it is necessary to know their natural history. They are, as they appear in theologic thought, the servants of satan. To find the origin of the idea of the devil we require to go back to the region of mythology. The idea of him had its birth in the experience which primitive man had of a power with which he had to struggle for physical life and for spiritual rightness. That power which lived in the stubborn earth, and against which (as it seemed to him) he had to work in his tillage, primitive man imagined as an evil power, an enemy of the sky or heaven power, the malignant cause of all human suffering. That power had its emissaries in all the forces with which man had to struggle ; the subtle forces perpetually waging wax against life in all forms and conditions. Invisible, but in continual activity, these hosts of evil operated throughout the world, making always for darkness, cold, and barrenness against the kindly hosts of light, heat, and fertility. They Trere the cause of the tempest and the blight ; winter was theirs, and the inclement season ; theirs also were disease, pain, and death. Such was the explanation which primitive man, in his ignorance, gave of the forces of Nature with which he had to struggle for food, shelter, and the conditions of happy life: they were evil beings, actuated by hate and malice. That explanation occurs in all the mythologies.

On being introduced into modem theology, witches took the place of demons in ancient theology. In the book of Enoch we have descriptions of demons in which there may be discerned the germs of later ideas of the angels of the devil, witches, etc. It represents them as the offspring of the sons of God, and the daughters of men. It gives their number as two hundred, and declares that they devour all which the labor of men produces, injure animals, and even kill and eat men. They taught sorcery and every species of iniquity, and for this Jehovah sent his holy angels to bind the chief demons hand and foot, and cast them into the lower depth of the fire, in torments and confinement to be shut up for ever. In the Talmud, which represents a large body of oral tradition which grew up in the Jewish Schools in Palestine and was continued long after the time of Christ, we find a development of demonology. In the cabalistic portion of the Talmud it is said—"All the spaces of creation are filled with good and bad spirits, these being divided into distinct orders having chiefs over them. The number of evil spirits, it is declared is incalculable. They swarm around every human being: a thousand on his right hand, ten thousand on his left. Their abode is a dark region under the moon. Their bodies are of water, fire, and air. They enjoy their meat and drink, and propagate their species after the manner of men."

In the dark ages, demonology became a pseudo-science. The schoolmen arranged the numbers and ranks of the demons, and the districts apportioned to the demon chief. They reckoned that the armed force of Lucifer comprised nearly two thousand four hundred legions, that is fourteen million, four hundred thousand. All these were to them veritable imps of Satan, creatures of flesh and blood regularly trained for their hellish war. It is their ideas to which Milton gave shape in "Paradise Lost."

It was common, then, for the preachers to declare that they had seen processions of damned souls, mounted on horses of fire, which hore them along with the speed of the whirlwind, and without a moment's rest, to the gates of flame. All that was to terrify the people into submission to the Church. The terror was carried into Protestantism. Martin Luther says in his "Table Talk"—"The devils are near us, and every moment ceaselessly plot against our life, health, and salvation. There are numerous devils in the woods, the waters, the deserts, in marshes and pools, lying in wait to injure human beings. Some there are in black and thick clouds occasioning thunder, lightning, hail, and storms ; they blight meadows and poison the air."

John Wesley was of Luther's opinion. He said that the giving up of belief in witchcraft is in effect giving up the Bible. Jonathan Edwards held the same sort of belief ; and Richard Baxter, whose writings were in the day of Burns the usual Sabbath reading—and were so till very lately—taught the same thing. Baxter took an active interest in the witch trials of his day, and believed in the confessions which the tortured creatures made. "Turn or burn," Baxter said to those whom he addressed.

Such then, is an outline of the natural and theologic history of "warlocks and witches," and by which it will be seen how deeply the idea of those beings as allies of the devil had entered into religious thought.

To sanction the belief, the theologian had but to quote the Levitical command, "Thou shalt not suffer a witch to live." The reading of that barbarous command as an order given by God was the fatal cause of the witch-burning in this and other countries ; but the command cannot reasonably be held to have been given by God. The persons called "witches" in the Bible were soothsayers. Their power to foretell the future and summon the shades from the world below was not doubted. They were credited with all the power of the Hebrew soothsayers ; but they were heathen, and might by their incantation seduce the worshippers of Jehovah ; and so the priests ordered them to be slain. The command is an illustration of Hebraic religious bigotry—a piece of priestly jealousy on the part of Hebrew priests. Walter Scott, though he took the orthodox view of the command concerning witches, admits that "there was no contract of subjection to a diabolic power, no infernal stamp or sign of such a fatal league, no revelings of satan and his hags, and no infliction of disease or misfortune upon good men" implied in the references to witches in Scripture. Indeed, it was not from the Bible that the idea of witches came which caused them to be regarded as servants of the devil and burnt as such, but from mediaeval speculation, based on the old nature-myths of evil agencies.

Now, in working our way out of this question of "warlocks and witches" there are two things to be apprehended ; first, that the idea of those persons as emissaries of satan is a modem survival of the old idea of evil forces in nature adverse to man. That superstition, taken up by orthodoxy, was formulated and presented in the creeds in the now familiar dogmas regarding the devil and hell. It was that superstition that Burns had in view when he lit up Alloway Kirk and showed the revel therein of the progeny of fanciful speculation.

Burns did not know what evolution has revealed to us. He did not know the facts that science has shown of the orderliness, lawfulness, and beneficence of the Power that works through nature. It is given to us to see that "evil is simply a temporary passing condition. . . . nothing more or less than mal-adjustment. The devil and sin and sorrow and calamity and sickness and tears and death all resolve themselves into this one word." But though Burns could not see this, he felt deeply the moral inconsistency of the idea of evil forces in nature with the idea of a good God, or the Over-ruler of nature and the Father of man. And he felt, too, how demoralizing in its influence on conduct was the superstition about "warlocks and witches." While men believed that they were surrounded and even possessed by beings who were the almost almighty agents of the devil, it was natural for them to feel that there was little use in struggling against adverse powers, that there was no possibility of high character open to them, that the burden of devilry was one which, in their fallen condition, they must needs carry. The devil was a most convenient excuse for all sorts of immorality : who, indeed, was there to blame for evil but him? If men were the children of the devil, ought they not to do justice to their parentage? Burns saw that the devil was a shelter to immorality that ought to be thrown down, and that it was necessary for the Church as a teacher of morality to lay the cause of evil where it ought to be laid ; viz., on ignorance of natural law, and mal-adjustment with natural forces. The entire brood of superstition flies at the touch A knowledge of natural causes, and the devil himself is dissolved in the process of human adjustment with the Power that works through nature, moulding man.

The other thing to be apprehended in clearing up this subject is that those who were regarded as "warlocks and witches" were the most advanced men and women of their station—seers, prophets, reformers in humble life ; radicals, protestants, heretics in relation to the "chief priests and pharisees" of their day. Had Mary Somerville, who mastered all the sciences ; Frances Power Cobbe, who, though deeply religious, cannot take the name Christian ; Mrs. Besant, who, while a devout and zealous servant of man, scorns the orthodox notion of serving God, lived two hundred years ago they certainly would have been burnt as witches. And had Hugh Miller, of Cromarty ; Thomas Edwards, of Banff ; and Robert Dick, of Thurso, been seventeenth-century men they would have been put to death as warlocks. Above all, if Charles Darwin had been a contemporary of Eichard Baxter, he would have been treated as the captain of the devil's host. The "warlocks and witches" were simply the martyrs of their day. The persecuting spirit of the Church had become so degraded that it seized on anything on which it could lay hands. Learning in those days was just beginning to be universal ; the democracy were commencing to think ; and the witch-hunt was the sport to which the degenerate sleuth-hounds of despotic power betook themselves. The whole proceedings against witchcraft were the clergy's retaliation on the democratic murmurs, criticisms, and insubordinations threatening to become dangerous to the influence of the Church. They were the answer of the presbyter (who was but priest in another form) to the desire for freedom of thought and conduct desired by the mass of the people. When woman sought wisdom at the doors of the Church she was made a witch. When the workman sought justice from the State he was treated as a warlock. They were made heretics and criminals for wanting to know, and for acting according to their highest reason. The struggling, strange, inquiring, thinking, and outspeaking men and women who were treated as sorcerers were actually the forerunners of the scientists of our day. They were students of nature, persons of singular elevation of thought, of extraordinary common sense, and of unusual virtue ; the leaders and redeemers of their class—none the less the soothsayers of the democracy though they were unconscious of having any extraordinary gift or call. The opposition which orthodoxy shows against science to-day is a survival of its treatment of witchcraft. It is, in fact, the old witch-burning in another form. The male or female heretic and reformer of to-day, who has to suffer clerical and social persecution, is simply the warlock or witch of yesterday.

All praise, then, to the courageous poet who wrote for us the parable of "Tam o' Shanter," and in Alloway's auld "haunted kirk," showed us the forms of the ecclesiastical spectres and social ghosts which still haunt the thought and life of to-day, and taught us to rise above superstition and slavery into the joyous light of knowledge and the sweet air of manly freedom. Through the bold humor of the poem, all the more effective though not openly declared, there shines the deeper lesson of the piece ; viz., that if men would have religion and morality made true and serviceable, the Church free from superstition, and the State free from tyranny, and every effort of the mass of the people to rise to higher life find ready aid in the powers that be, they must soberly, rationally, and devoutly give themselves to the pursuit of knowledge ; demand that those appointed to teach shall teach what is really true, that the pulpit shall stand for the high- est ideas and the surest facts, and that the minister of religion shall be one who can show men how to adjust themselves more harmoniously and vitally with the divine powers of life, so that mind, and heart, and soul, according well, may make one music of realized religion. And not only so, but they must demand of those who are set to rule that they rule righteously, not to favor any, but to serve all. So long as the people are sensual, the Church will be warranted in her superstition and the State in its despotism ; but when once the "Souter" and the "Farmer" become in earnest for a manly morality, both Church and State will be radically reformed.

A MEDIAEVAL TAM O' SHANTER.

ORIGIN OF BURNS'S GREAT CREATION.

BURNS is, of course, his own best commentator, and his original prose version of the Tam o' Shanter story, as contained in the letter to Captain Grose, throws the fullest light upon the poem. The letter proves that Burns's great creation has a higher truth than would have belonged to it had it contained more imagination and been less closely a transcript from country talk. Just by reason of its fidelity and its freedom from material embellishment, it possesses an historical value enhancing the admiration due to its luminous descriptive, narrative, and poetic power. Pegasus is not the less Pegasus because the poet chose to saddle and bridle him with facts. Leaving the pure wit and poetry out of account altogether, and considering Tam o' Shanter from a severely pedestrian standpoint, you find it a condensed but brilliant record of popular conceptions in demonology, witch- craft, and the ethics and practise of genial good- fellowship. Tom o' Shanter, in that aspect, is not Burns's ; it is Ayrshire folk-lore. It has, moreover, a moral, however subsidiary. The poet assures us in prose that the tailless mare served long as an awful example to Carrick farmers of the dangers of drink, and his verse closes with a quasi-serious and immortal exhortation on the same lines extended to the world at large.

Viewed in this sub-historical light as a document in folk-lore, and in its unique way a temperance lecture, the tale will repay a momentary survey of its supernatural characters. The witches. Burns scarcely tries to make grim ; they are grotesque. They are not Macbeth's sort. They are the witches of a dead creed. The belief which had so suddenly, late in the sixteenth century, attained such vast dimensions and caused so much barbarity had lost its power in little over a hundred years, and in two centuries was virtually extinct. The devil, the "touzie tyke, black, grim and large," sitting by his "winnock-bunker in the east," is rather a piece of comedy than of tragedy. He is only suggested, not full drawn ; but what there is of him is the devil of the late witchcraft period fallen upon evil times. He is not the full-blooded Puritan prince of the power of the air, and he is a strangely different being from the medieval fiend.

So much by way of preface to a legend of Ayrshire in the year 1290, which, in spite of the absence alike of mare and witches, yet presents remarkable features of analogy to the tale which Burns told forever in 1790. One must anticipate a different point of view and a different treatment. There will be no witches, for the thirteenth century did not take its witches over-seriously. The devil will perhaps have a graver object in life. But there will be, if not a Kyle or Carrick, at least a Cunningham drunkard ; there will be a Cunningham public-house, with its fireside ; and deep potations will still have the effect of conjuring up the devil—to act, however, the part of an apostle of temperance reform.

Historians have to thank the "Chronicle of Lanercost " for many a solid fact and many a queer, miraculous tale. A first-class record—the work of at least two authors (both probably Franciscan friars in Carlisle) its earlier half ending about 1296—is well spiced with marvels illustrative as often of the cantrips of demons as of the power of St. Francis and the Mother of Mercy. The second half, from 1296 to 1346, is so much occupied with Anglo-Scottish fight and foray, dealt with very competently more in the spirit of a man of arms that a man of prayer, that the satellites of Satan cease from troubling. The incident of 1290 is from the earlier half and from the miracle-loving hand. The friar, through his brotherhood, had excellent opportunities on both sides of the Border in the years of peace before the War of Independence. He had gleaned his information in many fields, and at least one notable confirmation of a contribution of his to Irish hagiology makes it possible to hold with strong probability that even his miracles are faithfully reflected from the gossip of his time.

Now to our tale. "For the sake of change of subject," says our holy friar in his annals of the year 1290, "there may here be related a thing that happened in Cunningham, in the kingdom of Scotland, which ought to terrify tavern-keepers and restrain drunkards. There was once—indeed there still survives, although now a changed man—a certain countryman of that province, William by name ; a man stuffed with riches, but unduly intent upon stuffing his stomach. Oh, how gluttony (*gula*) degrades and enslaves a man! He used to slink away from his own abode and into another district, because he could not have them at home, and would there consume in carousals and potations the goods of other men, until the hand of God laid hold of him in the following fashion. Once, as he sat alone beside the fire in the house of an innkeeper, he was rather devouring than drinking the ale he had bought, and when all the inmates of that house were busy at their work out-of-doors, there appeared to the foolish man the hideous figure of a spirit of the air sitting on the opposite side of the fire, with black body and ghastly face and fiery eyes of horrid magnitude. At sight of whom, the man of Bacchus was astonished, but, emboldened by liquor which sends the unarmed to battle, he began to inquire [of the figure] whose servant he was and what he wanted there. The other, with apparent pride, disdaining these demands, asked with a grin what person could be so very ill-informed as not to know him, the owner of a residence there, who for thirty years past, had held the foremost rank among the topers of the place. 'And to show that I do not deceive you,' he said, 'come and see what I have gathered here from the gluttony of ne'er-do-weels.' At once, William jumped across the fire and beheld by the side of the spirit of deceit a vessel so full of abominations as well-nigh to drive the fool demented. 'What you behold,' said the servant of iniquity, 'I have collected from the vomitings of your boon companions in your debauches.' Upon this, with his understanding awakened, which hitherto, as Solomon says, had not felt the rod ; and alive to his impending danger, he of his own free will uttered a vow to the Lord that never, under whatsoever necessity, for the remainder of his life, would he taste strong drink again ; which promise he still steadfastly keeps, to the wonder of all who had knowledge of him before. He acknowledges what he saw with his own eyes, and he related what is told above to two men of worth and credit with whom I was well acquainted."

The characteristics of the demon here make him explicitly the band of God. This is quite a normal mediaeval idea. Chaucer, in the Frere's tale, makes a fiend say of himself and his fellows :

"For som tyme we ben Goddes instruments
And menes to done his comandements."

The allegation of the devil, in our own Frere's tale, that he was the champion toper of the district, opens up too wide a field of investigation to pursue here. It may mean that the toper was dead, and that this was a devil-ghost of the "goblin-damned" type to which Hamlet feared his father's spirit might belong. Chaucer's above-quoted fiend says :

> "Som tyme we aryse
> With dede bodies in ful sondry wyse.

The devil in "Tarn o' Shanter" is of quite another order from that which William saw across the hearth in the middle of the tavern floor. The two have in common the fact that each is really the subjective creation of a mind inflamed by drink. Among some curious points of contact is the chronicler's observation on the courage-bestowing qualities of ale. *Audorcior ex potu* is as happy as Burns's own :

> "Inspiring bold John Barleycorn!
> What dangers thou canst make us scorn!"

And the picture of William, quizzing the devil as to who he was and what he was after, is as whimsical an incongruity as the free-and-easy greeting which Burns himself addressed to Death when he fore-gathered so memorably with him after a late sitting at Tarbolton.

"Wi' usquebae we'll face the devil!"

said Burns, and the saying is here completely vindicated.

The vessel of abominations is a realistic and positively Dantean touch, a very intense and powerful if coarse image, which will stand comparison with any in the catalogue of horrors in "Tam o' Shanter." It has the closest affinity to the lawyers' tongues and priests' hearts which the poet, on grounds not convincing, revised out of his poem. The reformation of William doubtless commended itself to the friar, as a fact admirably fitted to furnish a very proper and improving conclusion for the terrification of tavern- keepers and their too-sedulous customers. Tam o' Shanter, on the other hand—it would have been complete artistic ruin to reform him and Burns ; wisely and dramatically stopped short, leaving us to our own imaginings, if we feel the need of an anti-climax.

O thou! whatever title suit thee,
Auld Hornie, Satan, Nick, or Clootie,
Wha in yon cavern grim an' sootie,
Clos'd under hatches,
Spairges about the brunstane cootie,
To scaud poor wretches!
Hear me, auld Hangie, for a wee,

ADDRESS TO THE DEIL

AN' let poor damnèd bodies be;
I'm sure sma' pleasure it can gie,
Ev'n to a deil,
To skelp an' scaud poor dogs like me,
An' hear us squeal!

Lang syne, in Eden's bonnie yard,
When youthfu' lovers first were pair'd,
And all the soul of love they shar'd,
The raptur'd hour,
Sweet on the fragrant flow'ry swaird,
In shady bow'r;

Then you, ye auld snick-drawing dog!
Ye cam to Paradise incog.
An' play'd on man a cursed brogue,
(Black be you fa!)
An' gied the infant warld a shog,
'Maist run'd a'.

D'ye mind that day, when in a bizz,
Wi' reekit duds, an' reestit gizz,
Ye did present your smoutie phiz
'Mang better folk,
An' sklented on the man of Uz
Your spitefu' joke?

An' how ye gat him i' your thrall,
An' brak him out o' house an' hal',
While scabs an' blotches did him gall
Wi' bitter claw,
An' lows'd his ill-tongu'd wicked scawl,
Was warst ava?

But a' your doings to rehearse,
Your wily snares an' fechtin' fierce,
Sin' that day Michael did you pierce,
Down to this time,
Wad ding a' Lallan tongue, or Erse,
In prose or rhyme.

An' now, auld Cloots, I ken ye're thinkin',
A certain Bardie's rantin', drinkin',
Some luckless hour will send him linkin',
To your black pit;
But faith! he'll turn a corner jinkin',
An' cheat you yet.

But fare you weel, auld Nickie-ben!
O wad ye tak a thought an' men'!
Ye aiblins might—I dinna ken—
Still hae a stake:
I'm wae to think upo' yon den,
Ev'n for your sake!

www.ingramcontent.com/pod-product-compliance
Lightning Source LLC
LaVergne TN
LVHW051938100826
845154LV00016B/163/J

* 9 7 8 1 6 0 8 6 4 1 9 1 8 *